Lingo Dingo
and the
German chef

Written by Mark Pallis
Illustrated by James Cottell

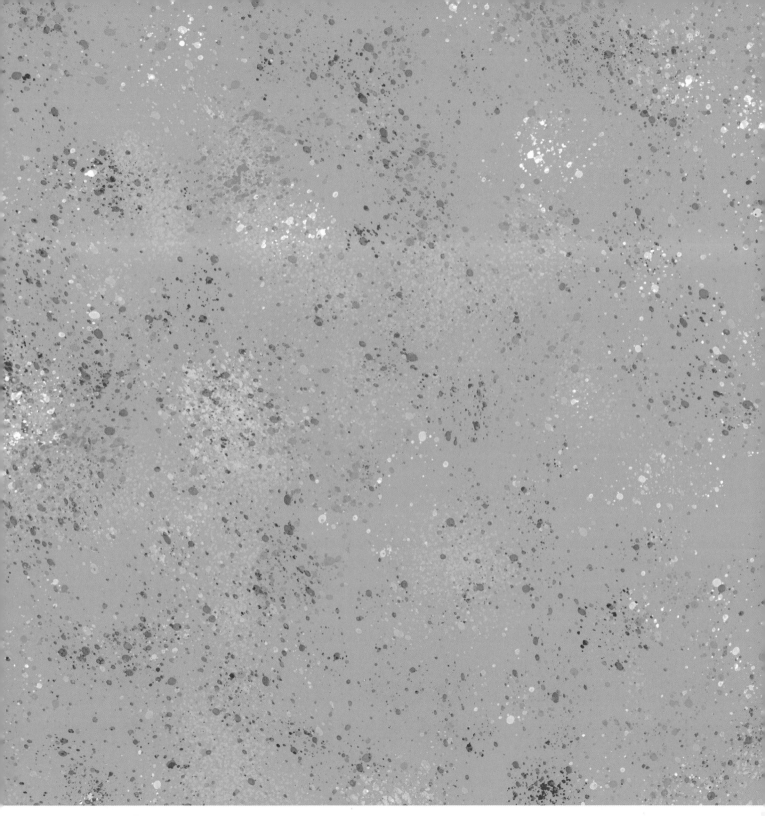

For my awesome sons - MP

For Leo and Juniper - JC

LINGO DINGO AND THE GERMAN CHEF

Story edited by Natascha Biebow, Blue Elephant Storyshaping
First Printing, 2021
ISBN: 978-1-913595-87-6
Ne uWestend Press

Lingo Dingo
and the
German chef

Written by Mark Pallis
Illustrated by James Cottell

NEU WESTEND
— PRESS —

This is Lingo. She's a Dingo and she loves helping.
Anyone. Anytime. Anyhow.

Lingo often helps her stylish neighbour Gunther, who lives by himself next door. She does a few jobs and has a nice chat. It makes Gunther feel good and it makes Lingo feel good too.

One day, Lingo arranged a special birthday party for Gunther. She even ordered a cake from a famous German chef.

There was a knock at the door, "It must be the cake!" said Lingo. But it was a monkey.

"Hallo. Mein Name ist Bäcker Nono. Ich habe ein Problem," he said.

Oh no. I can't speak German yet, thought Lingo. *Maybe 'Hallo' is like 'Hello'.*

Hallo = Hello; **Mein Name ist** = My name is; **Ich habe ein Problem** = I have a problem

"Hallo," said Lingo. Chef Nono replied slowly,
"Es tut mir Leid. Aber ich kann den Geburtstagskuchen nicht backen."

"I don't understand," said Lingo. "But let me guess. You want..."

Einen Wagen = a trolley; Eine Gewürzgurke = a gherkin;
Ballons = balloons; Nein = no

"Mein Ofen ist kaputt," explained Chef.
"Kann ich deinen Ofen benutzen?"

Chef's oven must be broken thought Lingo. "I know!
Let's bake the cake together," she said.

Mein Ofen = my oven; **ist** = is; **kaputt** = broken;
Kann ich = can i; **Kann ich deinen Ofen benutzen?** = can I use your oven?

Chef tapped his wrist. "Wie viel Uhr ist es? Neun Uhr? Zehn Uhr?" he asked.

Lingo pointed at her watch.

"Elf Uhr? Legen wir los! Schnell!"
They only had one hour until the party.

Wie viel Uhr ist es? = what time is it?; **Neun Uhr** = nine o'clock; **Zehn Uhr** = ten o'clock;
Elf Uhr = eleven o'clock; **Legen wir los** = let's go; **schnell** = quick

Chef Nono and Lingo whizzed around the kitchen:

Eine Schürze für dich.

Ein Schneebesen.

Eine Rührschüssel.

Eine Schürze = an apron; **für dich** = for you; **Ein Schneebesen** = a whisk
Eine Rührschüssel = a mixing bowl

"Reiche mir bitte
Butter, Zucker, Eier und Mehl," said Chef.

Lingo wasn't sure what those words meant, so she
just grabbed fish, coffee and onions instead.

"Fisch, Kaffee und Zwiebeln.
Ekelhaft!" laughed Chef.

Reiche mir = pass me; **Butter** = butter; **Zucker** = sugar; **Eier** = eggs; **und** = and;
Mehl = flour; **bitte** = please; **Fisch** = fish; **Kaffee** = coffee; **Zwiebeln** = onions; **ekelhaft** = disgusting

Chef plopped butter, sugar, eggs and flour into a bowl. "So that's what 'Butter, Zucker, Eier und Mehl' means!" laughed Lingo.

"Ich rühre, du rührst, wir rühren," said Chef and together they began to mix the cake.

Ich rühre = I mix; **du rührst** = you mix; **wir rühren** = we mix

"Und jetzt kommt Backpulver. Zwei Löffel voll," said Chef. Lingo guessed 'Backpulver' meant baking powder, but how much?

Before she could ask, Chef hurried away, saying, "Entschuldige, ich muss Pipi."

Lingo laughed, "I can guess what 'Pipi' means!"

Und = and; **jetzt kommt** = now comes; **Backpulver** = baking powder; **Zwei** = two; **Löffel voll** = spoonfulls; **Entschuldige** = excuse me; **ich muss Pipi** = I need to do a wee wee

I wonder if this is too much? thought Lingo as she added ten spoonfulls of 'Backpulver' to the mix.

She carefully put everything into the oven and before long, a sweet cakey smell filled the kitchen.

Backpulver = baking powder

"Was ist passiert? Der Kuchen ist riesig!" said Chef.

Lingo realised she had added too much baking powder.
"Sorry," she said sheepishly.

Was ist passiert? = what happened
Der Kuchen = the cake; **ist riesig** = is huge

They somehow got the cake out of the oven but ...

it was so big ...

... they couldn't hold it. "Disaster!" cried Lingo. "Eine Katastrophe!" wailed Chef.

Katastrophe = disaster

"I know what will make you feel better," said Lingo, kindly. 'Eat this 'Gewürzgurke'!"

"Ekelhaft. Ich hasse Gewürzgurken," said Chef.

They were running out of time.

Gewürzgurke = gherkin; ekelhaft = disgusting; Ich hasse = I hate

"I've got it! Gunther loves hats, so let's turn the cakey mess into a hat cake!" said Lingo.

First she shaped the cake, then she filled balloons with icing.

Next came the best part: POP! POP! POP!

It was a messy job but in the end, the cake looked fantastic.

"Rot, Orange, Gelb, Grün, Blau. Fantastisch!" said Chef.

Rot = red; **Orange** = orange; **Gelb** = yellow;
Grün = green; **Blau** = blue; **Fantastisch** = fantastic

There was a knock at the door.
"Die Tür!" said Chef.
It was Gunther, and he was wearing his special hat!

"Thank you. This makes me feel so special," said Gunther.
"You are special," replied Lingo.

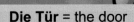

Die Tür = the door

Gunther was thrilled with his cake.

Chef's deep voice sang "Zum Geburtstag viel Glück…"

Zum Geburtstag viel Glück = happy birthday to you

"Pusten!" said Chef.

Gunther blew out all the candles in one puff and everyone tucked in.

Pusten = blow

"Ich esse, du isst, er isst, sie isst, sie essen," laughed Chef.
"Wir essen!" added Lingo proudly.

Ich esse = I eat; **du isst** = you eat; **er isst** = he eats;
sie isst = she eats; **sie essen** = they eat; **wir essen** = we eat

Everyone was happy.

"Ich bin glücklich,
du bist glücklich,
wir sind glücklich," cheered Chef.

Ich bin glücklich = I am happy; **du bist glücklich** = you are happy;

Baking a cake, helping a friend,
learning a new language... what a day!

But now it was time for bed. It was time to dream
about all the fun things that might happen tomorrow.

wir sind glücklich = we are happy

Learning to love languages

An additional language opens a child's mind, broadens their horizons and enriches their emotional life. Research has shown that the time between a child's birth and their sixth or seventh birthday is a "golden period" when they are most receptive to new languages. This is because they have an in-built ability to distinguish the sounds they hear and make sense of them. The Story-powered Language Learning Method taps into these natural abilities.

How the Story-powered language learning Method works

We create an emotionally engaging and funny story for children and adults to enjoy together, just like any other picture book. Studies show that social interaction, like enjoying a book together, is critical in language learning.

Through the story, we introduce a relatable character who speaks only in the new language. This helps build empathy and a positive attitude towards people who speak different languages. These are both important aspects in laying the foundations for lasting language acquisition in a child's life.

As the story progresses, the child naturally works with the characters to discover the meanings of a wide range of fun new words. Strategic use of humour ensures that this subconscious learning is rewarded with laughter; the child feels good and the first seeds of a lifelong love of languages are sown.

For more information and free learning resources visit www.markpallis.com

You can learn more words and phrases with these hilarious, heartwarming stories from NEU WESTEND — PRESS —

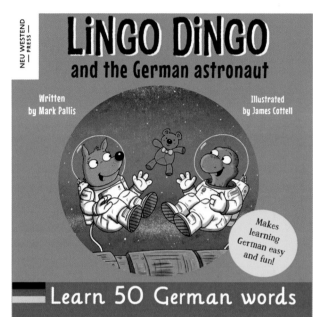

> "I want people to be so busy laughing, they don't realise they're learning!"
>
> Mark Pallis

Crab and Whale is the bestselling story of how a little Crab helps a big Whale. It's carefully designed to help even the most energetic children find a moment of calm and focus. It also includes a special mindful breathing exercise and affirmation for children. Also available in German as 'Krabbe und Wal'.

Featured as one of Mindful.org's
'Seven Mindful Children's books'

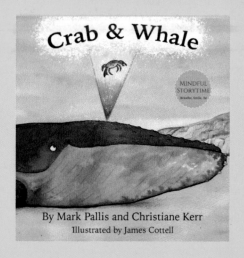

Do you call them hugs or cuddles?

In this funny, heartwarming story, you will laugh out loud as two loveable gibbons try to figure out if a hug is better than a cuddle and, in the process, learn how to get along.

A perfect story for anyone who loves a hug (or a cuddle!)

www.markpallis.com